PRIME

POETRY & CONVERSATION

L. LAMAR WILSON
RICKEY LAURENTIIS
SAEED JONES
PHILLIP B. WILLIAMS
DARREL ALEJANDRO HOLNES

INTRODUCED BY
JERICHO BROWN

SIBLING RIVALRY PRESS
ALEXANDER, ARKANSAS
WWW.SIBLINGRIVALRYPRESS.COM

Sibling Rivalry Press, LLC
13913 Magnolia Glen Drive
Alexander, AR 72002

info@siblingrivalrypress.com

www.siblingrivalrypress.com

ISBN: 978-1-937420-73-4

Library of Congress Control Number: 2014938399

First Sibling Rivalry Press Edition, June 2014

PRIME

INTRODUCTION: JERICHO BROWN

The first time I saw Nikki Giovanni give a public reading of her work, I was an undergrad at Dillard University in New Orleans, Louisiana. I remember a lot of what she said, but I sometimes wish I would forget her answer to a question someone in the audience asked just after the reading:

> Q: *What advice would you give to a young writer?*
> A: *Never say no.*

Giovanni's answer is the right answer, the truth. But I'll be damned if it ain't the hardest part of what we do when we make poems or when we contribute to any poetry community (whether it's by way of writing reviews or hosting readings or encouraging young poets who may or may not have a fingernail of talent).

The poet's life is not an easy life, for to live it well one must be prepared to follow the strangest and slightest notions, to take self-effacing risks, to jump off cliffs that are nowhere but in the mind. People look at you crazy because you feel all the bruises that come at the end of a plummet, but they don't see a single blemish. Don't believe me? Ask Adrienne Rich. In "When We Dead Awaken: Writing as Re-Vision," she says:

> For a poem to coalesce, for a character or an action to take shape, there has to be an imaginative transformation of reality which is in no way passive. And a certain freedom of the mind is needed, freedom to press on, to enter the currents of your thought like a glider

pilot, knowing that your motion can be sustained, that the buoyancy of your attention will not be suddenly snatched away. Moreover, if the imagination is to transcend and transform experience, it has to question, to challenge, to conceive of alternatives, perhaps to the very life you are living at that moment. You have to be free to play around with the notion that day might be night, love might be hate; nothing can be too sacred for the imagination to turn into its opposite or to call experimentally by another name. For writing is renaming.

In mid-December of 2011, *The Best American Poetry* Blog asked me to post something substantive every day for a week. And at the moment they asked, I was so mad at Nikki Giovanni that I didn't know what to do. In spite of the common desire to do nothing during the holidays but be drunk, I couldn't say no because it was an opportunity for me to take advantage of the *BAP* platform and ask some questions I thought the larger world should be asking. It was a chance for me to show others some work I had seen and loved and that I thought wasn't getting enough recognition. It was an opportunity for me to tell my man I love him and let the world know how much I try to make gratitude the center of my life.

As I write this, I am most grateful for the work of Darrel Alejandro Holmes, Saeed Jones, Rickey Laurentiis, Phillip B. Williams, and L. Lamar Wilson, the young, black, and gay men I referred to that week as The Phantastique 5.

When a group of black bodies stands
out from the rest and needs to be remembered
because they all resemble each other, some
use highlighters to brighten the black bodies . . .

These lines from Phillip B. Williams' "Manifesto" seem to me the best from which to begin a description of *Prime*. Over and again the work in this small anthology presents lawmaking lines of direct statement that ask the reader to re-envision the very act of reading and what that act means for subjective perception. What is text to those so often left out of literature? What is literature to those unwritten or written wrongly?

Throughout these poems, our eyes are turned toward so many objects we thought we knew, thought had seen properly. Now we face even the furniture that sits about us as if it is slanted and painted new colors until we have no choice but to re-see ourselves, or as Darrel Holnes would say, "Only the living have a reflection and you see yourself."

These poets are living indeed, and forging with each of their words the stuff of life, whether through complaint: "I'll tell you my problem/I'm a man who would love/ another man, whether/as a son, whether as a—" (Laurentiis) or ironic praise: "You cannot tell a soul/Must lie still   be quiet/Just take it like the man/You always wanted inside" (Wilson).

I am most taken, though, by how much these poems mean to participate in life to the point of being redeemed by that participation. These poets, in spite of being perfect candidates for that which is only academic and/or only conceptual, write as if poetry can speak directly to the soul, as if poetry is quite possibly the last hope they have to reach beyond themselves and touch anyone who perceives them:

> . . . Like a son rushing
> to his mother's stumble, the poet catches her
> as if his arms are the prayer's answer

& when her knees meet the earth
so do his . . .

(from "The Poet's Revolver Opens Its Mouth" by Saeed
Jones).

Prime is a lovely (and loving) book by five men bound
to change the way we read poetry because this is a book
of poetry by poets committed to allowing the poems they
write to change them. None of these poets ever say no.

Jericho Brown
Atlanta, Georgia
March 2014

PRIME

RICKEY LAURENTIIS

*And filled me
as no one will. As, even
I cannot fill
myself.*

Amiri Baraka

This is the story, as I know it.

Camille Rankine

CADAVER

I'll tell you my problem:
I'm a man who would love
another man, whether
as a son, whether as a—.

I've tried in fever
to defeat this, but in the act
I am defeated
like a fly knocking its head

against the glass.
Can't the fly ever know
to stop?—Or a man
who abandons his son,

can't he know it amounts
the same injury
to just kill the son instead?
Years

I've harbored, I've nursed this,
pregnant, fragile
as the earth must have felt
the time when I was buried in it.

Here's the grievers at the line,
their cries stiffening,
even the altar boys sniffling
against a prescription of manhood.
Here's the casket snapping shut,
a hiss . . .

       Who says that flesh softens at burial?
I cracked. I counted the flies in my wrist.

Black Iris
O'Keefe, 20th century, oil on canvas

Dark, imposing flesh. Darker still
its center, like the tongue of
a cow that has for a week now been
dead, spent during calf-birth, and the calf
still clinging to her, and his own tongue
wild for want of milk, and the calf
with flies in his eyes—*that* color: near-to-
purple, bruised. I should call it
beautiful, or beauty itself, this dark
room, broom closet, this nigger-dot.
I should want to fit into it, stand up in it,
rest, as would any beast inside a stable.
I should want to own it, force it mine,
to know it is my nature, and of
course don't I? Why shouldn't I want?

Black mirror. Space delicate
and cracked. Now anything could
go in there: a fist, veined, fat.
A body. And here runs the blood
through the body, deep, watery.
And here runs the message in the blood:
This is it—fuck her fag like you're supposed to.
And when the wind shakes
and when the iris shakes in it,
the lips of the flower shaping
to the thing that invades it, that will be
me, there, shaking, my voice shaking,
like the legs of the calf, who—out of fear?
out of duty?—is sitting by his dead
mother because what else will he do, what else has he?
Because a voice outside him makes him.

THIS PAIR THIS MARRIAGE OF TWO

Half-naked fevering standing
Up with a feather inked until it bled

Just above newly above the

Collarbone near the neck curved
There an apostrophe

Am I what that is that

Surface ekphrastic wrong to touch *But*
Touch me it begs so I try it extend a finger

Toward no real success

Must it be true
That everything I make will be a self

Eulogy for what it fails to be

A set of lines across the skin even
This dusky reflection I am myself looking

At this picture of myself made

Of metal and light light and glass it's there
I can see its strictness I can see

My eyes as ever haunted as the letter

O they are defining me this pair this marriage

Of two hollow suns but charged but
Can't a space be charged

With accent what creeps outside the
Visible what I see inside the mirror is it maybe

What I can't see what instead

I've been made to perceive
That voice colonial scribbled in wrong

Color twisted tones *You're such*

A problem child Whiten yourself
Straighten

Your speech but could it be

That what terrifies first is not
The image in the mirror but is the mirror

Fact that I can at all be

Reflected can be made to be seen and deeper
Than what I've been taught depth is

When I wrote

"I'm trying to write obsession into it" I meant
That deepness a reach toward a dead

Loss an understood failure

As when I had them scratch this dumb
Feather into my skin (*death, which is birds lifting*)

This feather I'm at pain

To touch as if communion were
True as if my body was true I was saying

I myself am

Too heavy am a screen too scored
To lift up—*But try it*

I think there might be pleasure

In this in failure might be a need for it
Is that why I'd stare at a burning cross two men

Burning at the edge of a field

Is that why when they're absent I invent them
Is that why I'm here

Companied with a surface an echo

Of myself locked with myself an X
I make and I make and I make

"Do not imagine

You can abdicate" a teacher once said
But to imagine sir

To imagine is the one mirror I trust

VANITAS WITH NEGRO BOY
Bailly, 17th century, oil on canvas

I'll show you a bone made to hold on to.
A pip. A dense fire in which once
the thinking imagination sprawled
like a breathing vine. He would put the skull
on the table (*And nearest to the worn
flowers, sir, or nearer to the flute?*) turned
just so so not to be too crude. That
was the boy's job, this cage with a debt
in it (*And whose boy am I, and what is
my name?*). Black erasing blackness,
body and backdrop: you are not permitted to enter
the question light asks of his skin as if it were
a field, a mind, a word inclined to be
entered. It's true: his face, his boyhood even
(*And what is my boyhood, and where is it from?*)
would fade if not for the rope of attention
yanked glittering across that face. Look.
This is my painting, my version of the Dutch
stilleven. I'm trying to write obsession
into it, and can. Open your eyes. Don't run.
Vanitas, from the Latin, for "emptiness,"
"meaningless"—but what nothing can exist
if thought does, if the drawn likeness of a bone
still exists? Why trust the Old Masters? Old
Masters, never trust me. Listen: each day
is a Negro boy, chained, slogging out of the waves,
panting, gripping the sum of his captain, the head,
ripped off, the blood purpling down, the red
hair flossed between the knuckles, swinging it
before him like judgment, saying to the mist,
then not, then quietly only to himself, *This is what
I'll do to you, what you dream I do, sir, if you like it.*

MEDITATION

Like noticing finally the non-wall
segregating night and day, we noticed what
light obsessed the canvas that,
no matter its severity, because of,
we always looked at, quickly,
never into, as if the light were some open secret
chastising us, telling us that this
world (the world, that is,
not the Earth) was made, in a way, to
terrify, that there is at least one thing in it, of it,
that won't properly relate: now a wall
won't meet the floor, now we're trapped
in a wheel, or gear of a clock, or car,
spinning, spinning just like the dream we have
of a free word, unproblematized,
unhinged from human desire, power,
a kidnapped-and-shackled-down version
of history, but only *like* that,
the shape before us being just a gear
(we think), or really just paint giving suggestion
of a gear, or oil, which is the smell of warm dirt
beneath our hungry hands.

PRIME

PHILLIP B. WILLIAMS

*If we must die
on the front line
don't let loneliness
kill us.*

ESSEX HEMPHILL

*The roof is made of stone. One by one the men unrobe. Even here
they cry like candles.*

QUAN BARRY

LEGACY

Foredoomed, I had a reflection. Cruelty
was its not wanting me—is
light skinning the body? Simply,
in his seeing was the frayed me, house un-selvaged by the
forced-together fitting. An energy
was unfixed in me, was chipped in
unpredictable ways, this burl a blight tricked into beauty, a
wood made to turn—no light; the body unseams itself. The man,
glass-caught, refused my broken civilization,
my iris a breaking wheel un-teaching joint from socket, where blood has
introduced itself to the exterior. I was not
afraid of being parted, was not shudder-hearted. Yet
the wheel landed, its woodwork applied. Altogether
skin abandoned bone, which shone a prayer. Was none corrupted.

MANIFESTO

I.

Words are black on this page.
Each character in a word is itself
a body. When reading these bodies
forming the words "black bodies"
one reads black bodies writing
black bodies. There are black bodies
on this page written by a black body.

II.

A book is a collection of black bodies.
Some are written by white hands. Some
white hands write black bodies without
mentioning that the bodies are black.
When writing a book one groups black
bodies together to make a point called an
argument, which is expected to put up a fight.

III.

When reading one views the black bodies
and interprets them, takes the information
they present and draws conclusions or
questions. Oftentimes black bodies
are misunderstood and revised for better
understanding. When one buys a book
one buys black bodies. One owns black bodies.

IV.

When a text is too difficult many slam
their books and do not return to the avoided
seeing, understanding, lack thereof. Checking
out books from the library is the rental
of many black bodies. They must be returned.
Keeping them equals theft. Damage
to the rented black bodies will result in a fine.

V.

When a group of black bodies stands
out from the rest and needs to be remembered
because they all resemble each other, some
use highlighters to brighten the black bodies
they have chosen as important. Others may
circle or underline, which marks up the book
of black bodies, ruins the collective.

VI.

Most people who write will write on a white
page but when a black body writes on a white
page it often goes unnoticed. When writing
a capital "I" the serif lines represent a pillar
which holds up the self. A held up self can hold
others up because it can't move and is therefore
reliably stationary. When writing "I" one must
never write "i" as it is a black body decapitated.
Either way the self must choose how to remain.

SONNET WITH A SLIT WRIST AND FLIES

I.
blade to the soft and the soft flashed open
    was the breakage of robins

II.
blood dripped to the bathroom floor
    splashed on the tile   painted a big toe

III.
the slit would talk back   sweet nothings in a red gown

IV.
wrist [rist] **noun** *1. the carpus or lower part of the forearm*
    where it joins the hand.

to explore the joint   window
        hinged on the edge
    of the body

        to slice it   to peek into the cut
and find the ribbon

V.
blood veined by the rhapsodic

VI.
a single mouth its total face

VII.
Risk [risk] **verb** *2. to expose to the chance of injury or loss;*
    hazard: to risk one's life

as the mind was made enterable   a boy stepped into
        was natural in him   was his
    and spectacular

VIII.

the heart's plucked quatrains   perfected through
    wreckage   a man waited in the pulse

IX.

a man found in the wrist who wanted out but
    who put him in?

X.

he spoke the four languages of the heart   he would
    touch   the boy   would

XI.

hurt the boy and translate his screams into a fifth vernacular

XII.

the boy he entered   was put into   no more
    than an   urn   than a tawdry vessel

XIII.

Sacrifice [sák-re-fise] **noun** *1. a giving up of something valued*
    for someone or something else considered
        to be of more value

the radius giving itself to the ulna
        the man   himself hidden
in the dark creases
    of vein-rope and contraction
            an artery's
        hierophant drum
the man

XIII.

stepped out of the dark and into where the cut
welcomed the bathroom's wattage

XIII.

stepped into the light his face a cut
a black hyphen from which all speech

XIII.

from which all darkness was made legible

XIII.

the single mouth his total face

XIII.

he would touch and call himself many names

XIII.

call himself a god but he was no god

XIII.

but was easy to believe him a god to walk to him to
relive how he got there

XIII.

stutter and suck

XIII.

was the sound of the wound closing in on them
both to hold them there

XIII.

as before in the dark when no one was around
blood wild with knowledge

XIII.

the man approached   was a knowledge himself
his face the one written page

XIII.

his option the sole option
he would take the boy
be mnemonic

be what had always been
prefaced to

he reached out
his hand

XIV.

and his fingers—thumbnail carving the boy's cheek—
touched   like flies

BLUE IN GREEN

A man become forest.
Thereafter the birds
of his shame defiled
his leaves. His veins
split mid-vine and
hardened into bark
after he'd hurt the boy.
Virtue: a pardon unhurried,
gotten to when the story-
book's refolded,
enchantment ending
as it began. Defilement.
And the boy ready
to axe each tree.
Not for vengeance. Not
because they reeked
berries, reeked justice.
The myth: birds startled the light
through the branches.
Bird startled bird.

OMEN ROUNDED WITH A SLEEP

Rain with his many hands over me: possession.
I unlatch my sternum for him to enter. My bones
drop to the floor and predict his touch—ten ravens
perch-hop-perched on the spine of a burning book.
A widow drives its loom, its silk-like stunned lightning
curtails the bedroom. I grab gossamer, pivot my wrists
to collect enough to fasten my tongue to memory.
When he rolls over my dreams play in reverse: a train
backs into the station; people walk out, their heels
pushing toward the turnstiles. But I can't make out
the station's name hidden behind the backs of many
heads: dark buds that won't bloom, won't stop
pursuing. Then a lone shadow cast by no one,
while what's unseen makes room for what's to come.

PRIME

DARREL ALEJANDRO HOLNES

I never see what has been done;
I only see what remains to be done.

BUDDHA

Everything dances against his body
because everything wants to plant something inside

MARCELO HERNANDEZ CASTILLO

CRISTO NEGRO DE PORTOBELO
for Oscar

It's when they see me naked that they finally believe
I'm from Panama. The crucifix
hanging on my black chest, underneath
the little hair I inherited from my father,
sweats as I perform what priests
and their laws call *unnatural acts.*
Only men grow body hair.
Only men are this dark and when
my hands finally darkened enough
to color even the blackest swans
I was sad to see them suddenly turn into wings,
plumed palms, hollow finger bones,
limp wrists. But then again, the struggle
of first flight against the moon's night
somehow was a freedom beyond heaven
or its wanting eternity. And now
rebellion is my new religion
or something else romantic and American
like a crownless king, perhaps an immigrant one
atop a throne, in native disguise.

THE DOWN LOW MESSIAHS

In his hands I was a cup overflowing with thirst—
finally in New York City, eager to bless his face
during this heat wave, eager to be a fire hydrant
holy grail. Sweet deliverance, this was my death,
salvation from his sins, from his woman
(and the ways she too *must* love)
as I wish I had been from mine—
A bath of silky steam fogs up the mirror, *see no evil*,
strong water pressure, hard rain, loud fall, *hear no evil.*
A small hotel room soap bar cleans off residue
left by his adhesive embrace of my lips
and washes my mouth out for *speaking evil*,
calling god's name out in vain again and again—
And here I am punishing myself for shining
the *other* light, here I am learning how to tell a lie.
But it's too late—we've bitten too many fruits
and cannot relearn the old world.
Skins stretching and sweat quenching
fire-starting words and worlds—
The half-made mold of her on his arms
cracking slightly when we embrace.
The virgin on my medallion hits my chest
each time I kneel in front of him
to pray. My ring finger slides *forbidden*
down his thighs in communion
with flesh, its burn and concurrent healing,
oh lord, its reddening appetite—

PHENOMENON
in memory of Adrienne Rich

Unable to see the rocks, we wreck
our yacht navigating
around your wedding ring to
waters in the moon's shadow.
Our bodies raise the tide until
we're chin deep, until we're submerged,
until we're mermen with armored bodies
and neither of us dare pull out
the bathtub's stop and let in dryness.
This undersea others assume has drowned us
has turned out to be the only place we survive.
So few men have gills, but each time I skip
a stone across a pond I wonder
if our ritual of diving into
the wreck is somewhat ordinary,
the drowned face still staring
toward the sun, evidence of damage worn
by salt and sway into this threadbare beauty,
disaster's ribs curving their assertion
among the haunters; we search the dark
for fragments to piece
a life together much as we would
with rubbish up top.
But when the dance of endless ripples
is much greater than the plunk
of the sinking stone, I know
this is more than mere sport—
somehow we've evolved
love to where it can glide
the rise and fall of life's constant wavering,
and not sink to the bottom when challenged

by nature. There's a reason we are rare.
One only reaches beyond when he confronts *nevers*
with perseverant *musts*, and look! Humidity in the air,
it's rising despite the pounding heat of a shining sun.
Rainbows arched across the sky—

I *Always Promised* I'd *Never Do Drag*

You liked me as *straight* as a man
in love with another could ever be,
and I did too. But you also loved
women, how their backs widen
where hips appear, how their necks
swerve like swans swallowing water
when they call your name,
their long hair stroking your face
as they wake from nestling
your chest the morning after.
So here I am wearing the wig I made
in the image of the blondes you preferred
but said you could never love, applying eyeliner
but not for it to run. *I will never*
love him again, I fearlessly announce to the mirror
as I beat my face with foundation base into submission,
as if one could ever fall out of the hero's arms
and not back into peril. Tonight,
for the first time, I dance to save myself
from distress, becoming the one woman
you'll never have instead. Tonight, at the Esta Noche bar
in the Lower East Side, I'm distance. The closest I ever came
to doing drag before was when I was crowned prom king
but chose instead the queen's tiara;
cubic zirconia somehow closer
to real than the king's cardboard cut-out crown.
Tonight I'm Diamante, extravaganza eleganza,
a gurl singing shine to the Yoncé record,
declaring myself Queen B of the Night, singing
take all, of me, I just want to be the girl you like, the kind of girl you like
sashay-shantae-strut-shimmy shining on stage,

dunking it like an Oreo, making the masses
shake they asses at the command
of the scepter firmly in my hand. A king,
I queen so hard my earth-quaking rule
breaks the laws of nature; flesh-colored spanx
and control-top leggings tuck it away
where the sun doesn't shine;
a black lace-up corset covers the missing rib
but lets the rest of me hang out enough to werk
and soak up applause from an audience
who loves this boy dressed as girl,
boy dressed as girly man, boy dressed as man
enough to drag, man dragging on,
man moving on, man gone.

STRANGER QUEEN

Beyond drag, she is a damsel tucking
to kick some ass as she crosses her legs
so tight in a flag that her bulge is the red barn

in the rural landscape painting, *American Gothic*,
where she is both husband and wife, or the missing
baby. She's another man trying to hide

what is inevitably bursting out, and perhaps
she transforms best by what she fails to conceal,
not folding into yet another norm,

poking out of the bandage, a beautiful bump
despite the tape, she's more than illusion, a real hybrid now,
wearing Helio's aureole diadem while overlooking the Atlantic

as she did on Olympus and in Rhodes, always the brazen giant
stealing light from father sun to be your motherland
incandescent, fertilizing this badland

with fluorescence. She's no queerer than the folk
you left behind, just modern enough to dress mess
and lip sync to the melody of engines.

She sings with grease,
she is the money-you-need mockingbird,
determined to get you into bed.

She's been hustling as long as the hour hand has held the clock.
She's chosen you to be the last minute. And desperate to swing for
a white-picket dream you kiss her spinning disco ball.

Only the living have a reflection and you see yourself
for the first time on her *espejitos* and dance surrounded
by dry ice, a new kind of smoke. You need this last chance

for romance. Hold her with your new language left hand and your
no one to speak it to right. Glide together as she asks you
to forget the navy blue rivers, the overcasts, the shade,

and forever bounce this lovelight between you two, a gospel
you believe; youth just looking for a nightlight, afraid of itself.
The music slows, but she keeps saying your name.

No one knows it back home, you say. She whispers,
You're in America now, slide in a little deeper. And then snap,
you're in it. But mosquitoes bite your flesh.

No, not bugs. Bullets hit you, thrown by bare hands
shooting to kill. They're not jealous of your freedom
or dance moves, but rather shoot to set you both free

from the prison of confusing this for paradise.
The garden's lock is broken; its gate hangs unhinged.
Dig your feet deep, Queenie, you must hold

the ever-growing world, under siege, on your shoulders.
Don't clean the soot off Old Glory. Don't bleach
her white stripes, or sterilize the rope we pull to raise

her body. All hail the peculiar fruit, and its dripping, bittersweet juice
burning our eyes as we fail to resist and reach for temptation
but then slip only to learn our falling is too some kind of grace.

PRIME

SAEED JONES

bend your knees because you want to,

not for any god or dirty nails in your shoulder.
go down knowing there is still a sky

to rise towards.

Danez Smith

Precision, pacing, placement, poise;
A sophisticated snap! is more than just noise.

Marlon Riggs

Scheherazade Sleeps Through the Executions

There are so many rooms inside her
& just as many locked doors, but sometimes

when the silence snaps shut, she hears the soft
thud. Another body falling onto the white

marble floor of her sleep. All night they fall.
She doesn't remember when the bodies started

disappearing from their lives & arriving
inside her, gagged & hooded, but she wakes

a little heavier each morning, a night's worth
of bullet casings tangled in her hair.

The King just now easing back
into bed beside her.

NOCTURNE: BEHEADED

All throat now   already brighter

than the stars.

I could hold you

in my song.   Sotto voce, tremble against me: a breeze

slips in, cools my blood
          to the color of garnet:

bed stained with stones,
          cold and finally useless.

I Orpheo,   I lyre. Down river, even damned

          with hum, there is room for your cry

in my mouth. Sweet, sweet sotto voce, I sang
          your moan until

the machete swung   then I kept singing. I eyeless,

I eternal.

          The guards hold blades to the sky
and cut the dark open.

          Do you hear me raining
from the wound?

My tongue is a kingdom.

You live there.

*A*UBADE

Two blind-folded men
try to waltz on the tips

of their toes. White shirts
full of breeze, hands behind

their backs. Polite partners.
The wind calls out each

step and, necks noosed,
they spin. Weak scaffold

creaking as they turn toward
the crowd, heads tilted

at the angle of spasm.
Lover, there is no one left

to tell us who we are
this morning. The bodies,

the bright smiles of the guards,
the men still in bed who hear

that same wind and let it
rake their sleep.

The Poet Puts a Gun
to Scheherazade's Head

& says, *Tell me where he put the bodies.*
Or, that's what he means to say, except

nerves have made an open grave
of his mouth & the hand holding

the gun won't stop shaking. He telegraphs
his question against the old woman's temple

with a tap-ta-tap-tap from his trembling
gun. This woman, long used to the demands

of desperate men with stuttering hands,
hears the question rapping against her skin

& looks out past the poet. A night sky
shot through with stars. Tap-ta-tap-tap

asks the poet again because he thinks
she didn't understand. One last look

at the sky & its dead gods. *We are,*
she sighs. *We are the bodies.*

THE POET'S REVOLVER OPENS ITS MOUTH

& Scheherazade falls as if struck by a sudden
need to pray. She sinks through the smell

of smoke & (the poet swears) there is an hour
between her body & the dirt. Enough time

for the wind to tighten its grip on her shawl
& promise not to let go. Like a son rushing

to his mother's stumble, the poet catches her
as if his arms are the prayer's answer

& when her knees meet the earth
so do his. The gun still in his hand,

he holds her as if the dead woman
will tell him what to do next.

PRIME

L. LAMAR WILSON

*the heart only beats
when locked in a cage
of bone.*

OCEAN VUONG

What was the price of your fear and your fist?

MELVIN DIXON

THE FIRST SHOWER

Ivory soap lathered
Dirt-caked & hay-slick, guiding
Mine, trembling & sodden, like
That heifer that slid from
Her mother's center into
Your arms hours ago. O
My sweet Daddy, such
Tenderness without desire
I've not known since, this
Lesson about what
Makes us different
How to keep it clean
How to hold it
Like a man   how
Did you know I'd never know
How to wield this gift
Like a blade
When to hold it close
When to turn it loose?

MALEVOLENCE

Only i missing here to make sense of it,
As in internecine, or interred, the deeper
Meaning of it all, bad news for every body.
How to step into its gays again & trade places
With its queens, its Madeas? You say it's always
The woman's fault anyway. It's always God's will.
Dear God, what made i scant, shunned? Of what man
& manner is i supposed to hate its selves this time?

O mi soul, who do you hate? Why can't you stop beating
Your meaty obsession with muscles & bears, lionizing
The easy pray, Jocastas and their pregnant pauses?
Prayer works only if you walk by sight, not blind faith,
& i will never fit this profile your i's write, that you
Expect our eyes to replicate in every body we write,
Our black market McCoyed. It's too heavy, hoping
This i broken enough for you & you & you
To enter. Chipola, Chattahoochee, Suwanee, Tallahatchie,
Jordan, Euphrates, Styx. *Ol' Man River, he keeps on . . .*

& i am bound to cross these on your bulbous buts, but i
Cannot bear this burden, these inches forecast, any longer,
The weight & carnage of water's audacity to keep flowing,
The human cargo, the marriage of breath & marrow,
Of hope snapped by the whir of a fan's blades
By the backs of a man's tied hands begging for
The father & the son & the holy bitch i refuse to call him.

& what do i know of wading, of the prick of death
Entered each time you's open your back doors?

Just a backwoods song as keepsake have i
To offer you. Listen while i show you you
in i. m a l e v   i   o l e n c e.

See our innards spilled on the turned page that tells
The same story you's wrote on the one before i
Fell in the deep end, black&bluesed & saw you corralled
In the continental shelf below i, blooming.

You should know i hate loving you.

You should know i will never stop.

CAKE
for Chris Brown

Rape doesn't happen to men
Not even boys if you know how
To spin your tale & feather it up
You're from that special, faraway place
It's different in the country
Just couldn't say no to it
Kind of, like, hot to trot
Like you're always on top
Of monstrous mounds of flesh
Eating away at the insides of
The pinkest part of you turned red
Rubbed long enough so that then
& only then *you can be a beast at it*
You can be the best at it
You cannot tell a soul
Must lie still   be quiet
Just take it like the man
You always wanted inside
You know you cannot live
Without it   the tale
Of all that steatopygia
Stroking your egos
Whose is it now   who's to blame
This burning   this desire to lie
About how the hunger became
A mirror you hate

AFTER THE VERDICT: MARSHALL, N.C., JULY 15, 2013

Let out the carpenter ant that cannot sleep,
That roves this sturdy glass, that oaken wall,
Licks the spots sugary hands & cloths have left

Let Venus alight smiles on the faces of
My brothers & sisters oceans away—
Their intemperate nights hewn

By Saturn. Let him blaze his rod,
Polaris flit & flaunt her somnolent
Cry: *This way, this way, this . . .*

Let blue royal & fuchsia kiss
Bloody pistil, its wingéd eyes
A wound wound about golden bulbs.

Let this therianthropic soul be born
Again in you, skylight. Let all mask
This comedy of errors we call America.

For each cloud has become a lone
White hoodie, each a shroud
As the children wonder aloud:

Why won't God stop crying?

Mothers, struck dumb, comb their hair,
Cook grits, turn on the TV, let SpongeBob
Do his queer work with time.

Let us reach for the poster of Obama
Above the sill, all glitter & golden.
How gay he looks, this new black vision

Of beauty, this man women & men of all hues
Ogled as they sloped into booths, their wombs
& manhoods aching for birthrights renewed.

& then, we saw a rainbow, I swear, but
By the time, we found our cameras, it was gone,
Lost in a game of Russian roulette. Now turn

On the news again, listen as another lawyer says,
He was nice to her, a surprise defense for any black boy
Walking home alone, of a too-black girl, smitten,

Her face round, eyes too full of joy, dumbfounding heads
Talking shit, trying to find pity where none resides. Who will decipher
Her language, forgotten by even those as dark & diasporic as she?

& could you fight for him, our son Trayvon, if he'd been like me,
If rainbows were flags he dared to don as a shawl? Could you
Mourn that part of him lost, too? Or been tacitly relieved

He didn't live to shame you? David Kato?
Marco McMillian? Dwayne Jones?
Mark Carson? Remember them, don't you?

Listen now as a cat mews & paws at the ant
Roving on this glass. Listen as a train squeals
To a halt, its ache a beacon of our undoing.

We cannot let them in this tale, for pity's sake, for
Behind the fog, over the horizon, this mountain, rainbow,
The drumline on those tracks—we are the drummers—

Who lies at the end of this tunnel vision? What
Peace found in all these rivers of our children's blood?
No light there before us, only hissing & gnashing,

Another dead black boy's flesh, our daily bread.
Let us sit at the table of brother & sister hoods, you say,
Let us feast, no, *beast it, beast it, beast it, beast* . . . Let us

Mark our words, mine what we mind, for whatever we say,
No words will bring them back, none absolve the guilt, all
This affluenza, this blood on your hands, Lady Lazarus.

& yet the lark never forgets her morning assignment, not
Before or since that august night, the first black first family
Holding hands in a Chicago park. O bloody Chicago,

Another city fashioned by a black man's mined mind.
Don't you remember? We saw a new heaven
& a new Earth, I swear, & then it was gone.

ON THE OCCASION OF *MY FORTUNATE ESCAPE*

Do not look for me at the front of the church,
In a white box, smile pressed into the corners

Of my mouth. Do not expect me shorn properly
& slicked into a fresh-pressed, respectable suit.

Do not seek the silent reflection or comfort
Of a creaky pew & a good old hymn. Go

Instead to the darkest alley you can find
On Main Street. Talk to the man who listened

To the wonders of my day, as if fairytale,
Who shared my bed at least twice a month.

Mention my name & watch his eyes alight
With the taste of four-cheese macaroni

& artichoke-spinach dip. Undress as he recounts
The amazing grace of the nape of my neck,

The briny eyespit caked there. When
he falls into you & calls my name, give thanks.

PRIME

CONVERSATION

And when we speak we are afraid
our words will not be heard
nor welcomed
but when we are silent
we are still afraid.
So it is better to speak
remembering
we were never meant to survive.

AUDRE LORDE

CONVERSATION: DARREL ALEJANDRO HOLNES
& L. LAMAR WILSON (DECEMBER 2013)

Darrel: Poems in your book intersect disability poetics with the black, queer, Southern experience. What was that journey like? To write about the body like many queer poets do, but also a body that is "disabled"?

Lamar: I honestly had a joy-filled childhood. I'm always disappointed that *Sacrilegion* does not capture that joy as much as I'd have liked. I grew up in neighborhoods called Long Bottom and Burden Hill, full of sage elderly people, men and women who endured the horrors of Jim Crow and the Depression but emerged with a deep-seated faith and empathy for others. They took care of one another. I have always been fed by the love that they poured into me and into one another. At the same time, I held within me a deep sadness with which I wrestle at all times because I was born into a body that defied what I felt inside. I could hear whole symphonies that I wanted to write and play that I could write as a classically-trained musician but that I could not fully play (on all of the instruments) because of my paralysis. I know, that's ambitious, wanting to be able to master all instruments instead of just my trumpet. However, that's just the kind of person I have always been, one who wanted to be the best at everything, and the musical artists I admire mastered and played many instruments on their projects.

Darrel: Is that why the poems are at once at the intersection of history and individual self? Was it your goal to "transcend"?

Lamar: I don't think we can transcend the self. That is never the goal of my poetics. Living with a physical difference that the world sees and names a "disability," you come to accept that your life as you live it is one thing, that the historicizing of your identities will be defined by others in ways that you can't control. But what you can control—which is the journey of *Sacrilegion* and of my daily lived experience—is how you respond to that imposition of naming, what you answer to, who *you* say that you are. *Sacrilegion* was my way of revisiting the shame I internalized, living with a hand that years of prayer and "laying on of hands" by ministers and doctors didn't heal. We are taught to hide our imperfections, to medicate them away, to buy things that obfuscate them, but I never was able to nor did I desire to live in that kind of denial. I could not hide my paralysis, and on a related note, I could not hide my queerness, which many align with some kind of "disability," though I do not. It's not always easy dealing with other's ignorance and projections of hatred, and in many ways, I internalized other's shame about my queerness, too. So I, instead of hiding, swaddled myself in, no, armed myself with, language—that of the Church, that of various culture's literatures (novels first, then essays, then poems and plays)—that helped me feel freer, empowered, more than what others saw and said I was and could be.

I flourished as a child in every way: academics, sports (primarily tennis), religious organizations, etcetera. I felt, despite what they saw, I had God's "favor" and grace and believed what I was taught, that with God, "all things are possible." But when I first kissed a man, I felt I had betrayed a pact I made with God, never to sin *that* sin, never to succumb to that which in black communities at that time was the worst crime against humanity and one's self one could commit. *Sacrilegion* was also about my redefining my relationship to God and that warped theology, to choose and define a theology of liberation, self-acceptance, and reverence for all life as it manifests, including my body and all of its scars and all of its erotic power.

I see you wrestling with this commingling of desire for God and for that which some call "unnatural acts," especially in "Down Low Messiahs" and "Cristo Negro de Portobelo," brave, powerful, and necessary poems. What was your experience with faith in Panama? And how did your experience as a queer immigrant, seeking love in such a wild kingdom as New York City, shape that poem and others we see in *Prime*?

Darrel: Hmm . . . My adult journey with faith really started when I came to the United States, so some of my poems have an FOB (Fresh Off the Boat, as in recently immigrated), point of view because though familiar, it still feels foreign . . . that which *is* natural, some call "unnatural acts," as I wrote in "Cristo Negro de Portobelo." That poem is as much about points of view as it is about acts, be they natural or unnatural.

Lamar: Interesting. How, then, does one distinguish it from performance, from, shall we say, religious drag? What truth do you find in it? And, more importantly, how do you find the parallels of worship of God and of another's body useful for your poetics? You really meld them beautifully!

Darrel: "Cristo Negro . . ." is probably my most Panama-oriented poem (The Black Christ or "Cristo Negro" is a celebrated Catholic icon in the town of Portobelo, Panama), where spirituality is both mine and "theirs," the "they" being these priests. When I say "unnatural acts," I think about the latter part of that phrase, "acts," because it could be read as acts that defy nature, as though the "act" itself is the impossible becoming possible. "Unnatural acts" should be read multiple ways. There's more to it than the "freak of nature" association, as if I'm breaking some rule. Rather in my poems I'm bending physics into a new realm where these acts happen. In a way it's not about natural vs.

unnatural, but "whose nature"? Does this come from a place where such love is possible and real? Making the impossible possible is the mission of love in "Phenomenon."

Lamar: Why then mark them unnatural and "other" them? What critiques can one deploy by interrogating these negative connotations? I ask because I also chose to take this language that is designed to demean in *Sacrilegion* and in "Malevolence," an excerpt from a larger project about the violence we do to one another in our words, in our most intimate acts.

Darrel: Well, let me see. There's religious drag, as you say, and there's this pos/neg language thing. Let me address the latter first. I think the world is changing, acts that might have been unnatural or dubbed as such are part of a new nature (at least in terms of them being mainstream), and in a way their way of defying nature—abomination is too violent of a word—is how we know it belongs in this new world, so I don't see naming or othering as negative anymore, but rather just as affirmation that whatever is being "othered" is what it needs to be because it's an avenue to a new world, to a new faith.

And religious drag, perhaps is a way of transitioning. I mean it's what Catholicism did in Latin America, even worldwide—the Church put the Virgin Mary's veil on other deities to shepherd people away from "paganism" and into the Church. I don't think this was trickery or deception. I just think of this as transition, and I think we are transitioning into a consciousness beyond love/lust as procreation, threatened by homosexuality or any other sexuality or love dynamic. I think now is about compassion and tolerance, which necessitates more mainstream variety. And this religious drag is a way to transition as it allows us to see all the layers at play at once. We have to see the layers because it's all about being awakened to them, that's from where compassion and tolerance comes, when we can see and love both what's common at the core of it all, and also how each piece stemming from that core is different.

Lamar: Asé. Though I do think the "they"s who were white religious missionaries did not understand or believe that their Christianity is a descendant of a number of ancient religions. And, in many ways, a new wave of faith-filled people, understanding intimately these intersections, are drawing on a number of traditions as they connect to their sense of the multitudinous valences of the force called, in English, God.

Darrel: Right. I had multitudinous valences in mind in the poem "Stranger Queen." The Statue of Liberty is a recreation of several other statues that have existed since the ancient world, always gatekeepers but referencing different religions, ideologies, myths, and politics of the time. This figure, like religion, has evolved, and that's beautiful; the faith, this figure, stayed the same though sometimes male, sometimes female. My stranger queen is both because she is now, history, and future potential. At first, I thought we'd always be bound to time and space because language is in the here and now, but poetry's job is to reveal the limitation of language, and by this suggest there is so much more that cannot be said but must be felt. Theater does this, too, it exists to provoke. It hopes its words help its reader or listener *feel* the journey of discovery they are on, awaken to it.

Can you tell me about the sense of self in the poem, "Malevolence"? There is the little "i" and the "soul" and the speaker. Is this voiced by the individual or some sort of abstract or collective?

Lamar: The act of writing and the words one chooses, while liberating for the self, can simultaneously hurt any number of people. Men, in particular, are guilty of using words in ways that are "internecine," as the poem says, that simultaneously do harm to themselves and others, words that are patently toxic and destructive. It is men's words, after all, that often start and drive wars. "Malevolence" is, I suppose then, an abstract meditation on my relationship as a queer man, often not afforded a certain kind of masculinity, to this violence. I find *this* relationship to language unnatural, learned. I believe we learn, as men, that we are to speak a certain kind of way to assert ourselves, affirm the authority of our phalluses. As an avowed womanist, I am deeply disturbed by what I have learned I *must* say, if I'm to be seen as an "alpha male," which is the masculinity held in highest regard. It is this masculinity I'm expected to perform, or the femininity I'm expected to dissect and extract from the self I reveal in my poetics.

Darrel: The poet who writes with poison words?

Lamar: Well, they may not "poison," but they definitely can be "injurious." Black men, in particular, are in this fight over our words. Still. Just look at the discourse between two of our elders, Amiri Baraka and Charles Rowell, about Rowell's anthology, *Angles of Ascent*. So much of that, I sensed, was tied up in ideas about who should be able to decide whose words, and whose valences on blackness, are canonized for the ages. We are constantly wrestling with ourselves. With each other. Terrance Hayes, Major Jackson, A. Van Jordan, Thomas Sayers Ellis, Carl Phillips. All these writers have resisted and/or interrogated the performance of a certain kind of masculinity in their work, with great success, and I see those of us who Sibling Rivalry Press and Jericho have collected here (and others who are publishing amazing work) as challenging this *expectation* of a certain kind of wrestling, a certain kind of fighting. I think that's the genius of what Adrian Matejka did with bringing the metaphor that is prize fighter Jack Johnson to life in his latest work and why *The Big Smoke* is getting all the praise it so rightly deserves. It is also the reason that one of my sheroes is Phillis Wheatley. She chose to put herself in conversation with the white men she is now too often accused of "imitating." I see her critiquing their ideas, even as she embraces their God, throughout *Poems on Various Subjects, Religious and Moral*.

Darrel: Are you saying that your work is preoccupied with this fight? Your work seems to go beyond this.

Lamar: Thanks, I sure hope that it does. Malevolence is defined as acting with a desire to harm another person. It dates to the 15th century, which is, for some, the dawn of the modern era. The poem with that title, which set off a number of others you see, aims to turn the mirror away from a number of speakers' earnest, confessional "i"s. This approach to the "i" is, I sense, eschewed in the contemporary poetic moment. This sincerity, ironically, so shaped *Sacrilegion* that I never thought it would be published.

These new poems put this "i," lowercased as a meditation on this belittling, back on the "you" (the reader, the literary journal editor, the book publisher seeking "The Next Big Thing/Voice"), who brings to any poem any number of expectations that have particularly been ascribed to writers who are marked black and male. These poems wonder: Why are black boys and men seen as malevolent beings— historically and in the present moment? The Trayvon Martin case and the troubling figure that pop star Chris Brown is, which "After the Verdict" and "Cake" engage, respectively, remind us that this trope is not old news.

Now, I would be lying if I said that I—L. Lamar Wilson—was not in these new poems. I have endured a great deal of malevolence, and as I thought about my experiences and realized that adding "i" to "malevolence" spelled "male violence," a whole world of poetic possibility opened up to me. Yet, I am reaching, with these poems, as much as I can beyond my autobiography for something meditative, mythic, and timeless. Those raised by women singularly as well as those, like me, who have loving relationships with their birth fathers and any number of men who helped in their rearing, and yet have a woman-centered way of being and seeing, endure a great deal of personal and social malevolence. We also have to look into the mirror at our own malevolent acts, those we exact on ourselves and others, how our same-sex intimacies blur the lines between pleasure and pain, how, as I've said, the words we write can bring pleasure and do great harm. At the same damn time. How can any of us—black, white, or other, male, female, or in between—escape or, as you say, transcend violence?

To that end, I am, admittedly, very nervous about these five poems because they are still so new. They don't feel "done" at all and have not been vetted in the ways we are accustomed, and as you saw with *Sacrilegion*, I work so hard to ensure that poems not only stand alone, but also speak to one another to tell a collective story that people can enter and engage. Accessibility does matter to me, and I'm not yet sure how accessible these poems are.

You, on the other hand, manage this simultaneous sharing of a speaker's self and of putting a mirror up to the reader in "Stranger Queen" and the rest of your work in this collection. How did you decide to make use of ancient myth as you meditated on the life of the contemporary drag queen? What do you make of the role of the violence of which I speak (linguistic, sexual, social) in your work?

Darrel: The violence you speak of saddens me, and I grieve for all of my brothers and sisters who fall victim to humanity's vices. I'm interested in postcolonial theory as a transnational being. For me, being a transnational being, or a kind of constant immigrant, means that I'm always at the intersection of many national identities. Initially I wanted to queer the concept of a stranger king as a way to flip the bird to this sexist, racist theory. A stranger king is a concept from colonial discourse whereby a foreign ruler is peacefully accepted by a people as a means of conflict resolution. My impulse to write the poem was reactionary, but then it became something else. I think I looked to the root of this thought and discovered so many others. I discovered there are multiple sides to this source, and then I saw her, the Stranger Queen. And all my ideas of transnationalism and postcolonial theory, religious and political drag came crashing together. The piece exists to stimulate people's thoughts about how all this fits together. There's a harmony, whether or not you like the song. So I won't make an argument for the piece because it's not about a single point of view, but really a "manyness" about how past potentials and future potentials are simultaneous, not linear. In other words, our past isn't "behind us" but rather ever present in the now.

The statue wears Aureola's radiant crown, she is the Colossus of Rhodes, she is a 19th-century black woman (the original model for the statue was a black woman in France), and also a Mediterranean goddess—she is ancient yet modern. What's curious to me is that the idea of her as transgender or a man in drag feels as though it came out of thin air. I did set out to queer the stranger king, but I was going to make her all woman, a stranger queen, but she came out, birthed through me, as a stranger *queen* —both genders as if to bring together a male and female consciousness.

To your point about hurtful language, I think awareness is healing. So if you've been hurt by the language of men, or the ruler, or the colonizer, you must become aware that the sword swings both ways and has two blades; this pain is also empowering. Take that power and heal yourself. That's what this poem ultimately became for me. By its end I had healed; I had forgiven.

Lamar: You know, since you bring up the theory that interests you, womanism is the only theory that feels right as I meditate on what informs my poetics. "Black male feminism," as it is often called, still grapples with affirming masculinity while acknowledging the challenges women face. Womanism—by putting the bearer of new life and possibilities at the center of a community that desires equality, symbiosis, and respect for and among all of nature, human and other—disrupts the imposition of masculinity and chauvinism in the world. It allows for whatever is along various prisms of identity *to be* in all of their gradations. It is no wonder, then, that womanism largely has been written off since Alice Walker challenged us to embrace it three decades ago, and it is no wonder that I would embrace that which is cast aside or unpopular. But enough about theory.

My poetics is not only about the challenges of the disabled and of being born of the rural, hyper-religious South. I am interested in people, life forces, and ideas that we ignore and/or abhor, those that are not actually silent, but rather marginalized so much that they are in a conversation with themselves on the periphery. I like to hang out among them and glean the wisdom, critiques, and insights they have to offer those who have the microphone and the attention of the masses. All the poets *Sacrilegion*'s poems explicitly name themselves having been written after—Ai, Sterling Brown, Lucille Clifton, chief among them—mastered the art of giving voice to those *not* "voiceless," a framing I find disturbing, but those whose voices have been ignored.

I should say, too, though, that I think more born in America need to acknowledge that we are all transnational bodies. We are all descendants of immigrants. It's simply that some of our ancestors got here sooner than others. That of which you speak is quite relevant to both the 21st-century immigrant and the 21st-century progeny of 18th- and 19th-century immigrants, those who came by choice and by force.

Darrel: I love how theory is a way for us to put a grid on this and chart it for our readers, but I want to underscore the point that all that of which I speak is dynamic and everyone experiences it on an individual level according to their levels of awareness. And that by surrendering the comforts of theory and history we release our "unknowing" to know that it's all uncertainty in that it can never be boxed, defined, or pinned down. I'm not about these systems. I'm about transcendence, and that's something theory isn't because this can only be felt and known, not spoken or studied.

Lamar: Why is transcendence important to you? And how do you define it precisely? As I've said, my embodied experience complicates my experience with and understanding of one's ability (or even necessity) to transcend. I think poetry helps us expand, better understand, feel, and empathize more of and beyond our selves, but not transcend them. I want to transcend! Teach me how your poetry can help me (and others) do so. I want to believe it is possible.

Darrel: I think right now to transcend means to be aware and to reconcile our present self with all that it is composed of. I think right now so many of us look in the mirror and only see the surface. Sure, since the Renaissance and even far before there's been this idea of the "self" or the "soul" in world literatures, but when I look in the mirror, I see a projection of light at an intersection of everything that makes me what is, in that moment, reflected in the mirror; quickly changing and simultaneously alive and present in its other incarnations whether or not my eyes can see it right then. The Stranger Queen, s/he is a stripe of color revealed by the prism. Transcendence is the light and living limitlessly. That's what my poetry is for me, a part of my illumination, a part of my being, a part of being.

CONVERSATION: SAEED JONES & PHILLIP B. WILLIAMS (OCTOBER 2013)

Phillip: Recently the idea of having a mentor crept up, maybe a couple of days ago, when I introduced one of my cohorts in the MFA program to Essex Hemphill. I could be exaggerating but it seemed to me that a light came on inside him. We were in the library browsing and being entirely too loud when he asked for a suggestion and Hemphill's *Ceremonies* seemed to just lift from the shelf. For me, *Ceremonies* was a defining text. It gave me a foundation of audacity: I can write about being black, queer, afraid, angry, urban, lonely—I'm sure I wouldn't be writing if it weren't for him, for his work. I do consider him a mentor even though he had no bodily presence in my life.

Saeed: One of the *very* few images from the Bible that have stuck with me, in spite of my upbringing and continued practice as a Nichiren Buddhist, is the light that struck Paul on his way to Damascus. That's how I feel whenever I'm introduced to a mentor on the page, like I've been struck not by lightning, but something brighter: a sense that my understanding of writing, or even better, what it means to write my way into and through this world has changed.

In college, I was introduced to Essex's poetry while watching the film *Brother to Brother*. In one of the early scenes, a character recites one of Essex's lines: "Some of the men we love are terrorists." I remember sitting in my dorm room, curled up on my bed under my Walmart-bought blanket and there, with those words, was that light. I sat right up! It's so powerful to come across poetry that absolutely speaks to your life across time.

In college, I really struggled with internalized homophobia which manifested, most visibly, in my insistent attraction to "straight" men who were often at best delusional and at worst dangerous. It almost cost me my life at one point. At the time, though I vaguely understood what was happening and why I was making the choices I was making, I didn't quite have the language, and then boom—"Some of the men we love are terrorists." As is so often the case in Essex Hemphill's writing, a single sentence can illuminate an incredibly complex and volatile dynamic. I could read and think about the world of that sentence all night.

That sentence introduced me to a crucial mentor, someone who gave me a blueprint for saving my own life and translating that experience into poetry of my own. What's frustrating though, is that it took so long for me to come across his work. Sure, I could (and should) have been a more studious researcher of black queer poetry, but there's also the issue of erasure. The work of so many would-be "mentors on the page" for black queer writers is out of print, forgotten, and all too rarely resurrected. So I think a conversation about these mentors is also a conversation about erasure and recovery.

Phillip: And not just of those texts but also of the self, our selves in particular, and the many selves of others in a general sense. I think of my recent discovery of Melvin Dixon's work. I can't remember how I came across it but L. Lamar Wilson mentioned him in a conversation once, and I hadn't looked him up immediately. Then, just browsing the online archives at my school, I came across his name and his two books of poems that were online. At the end of his second poetry collection, *Love's Instruments*, Melvin Dixon shared in his speech at OutWrite 1992:

Although I still find it difficult to imagine a glorious future for gay publishing, that does not mean I cannot offer some concrete suggestion to ensure that a future does exist.

First, reaffirm the importance of cultural diversity in our community. Second, preserve our literary heritage by posthumous publications and reprints, and third, establish grants and fellowships to ensure that our literary history is written and passed on to others. I don't think these comments are bleak, but they should remind us of one thing: We alone are responsible for the preservation and future of our literature.

If we don't buy our books, they won't get published. If we don't talk about our books, they won't get reviewed. If we don't write our books, they won't get written.

The conversation of erasure seems to always be in the air. Who remembers whom and in what way? Who is responsible for memory? Like Hemphill, Dixon was lost to complications with AIDS, which has been one of the largest erasers queer men have ever had to face. The very last sentence of Dixon's speech was "You, then, are charged by the possibility of your good health, by the broadness of your vision, to remember us."

Something that is powerful about Jericho getting us together is the legacy of memory, of creating a space where we as young poets can be remembered in the immediacy of our present time without the need for us to die or be exhumed by means of our texts being posthumously published. We are not out of print, are hardly in print, but the stage that we've been given was never given to those who came before us at such an early point in their careers or if ever in their careers. It's a way that erasure can be resisted by investing in the present and instilling in the youngest of us a resistance to becoming necromancers of the self. We shouldn't have to die in any way in order to live, to be heard. And in our youth we are tasked with recovering those who have left this world unheard, ignored, victimized, stigmatized, buried, out of print, and out of history.

Saeed: I absolutely agree. But I'd also like to emphasize that I don't think of this as a burden or even a "responsibility." This is a joy. A necessary joy but a joy all the same. When I am in the company of my brothers, near and far, past and present, in person and on the page, I am home.

Phillip: How do we define home? I guess I am also thinking about how writing is a way of creating a home space. This is not to suggest that there is safety in writing; however, I do think that there is a type of phoning home, a tapping into a space where interior feelings and thoughts can be turned into something more tangible and therefore inhabitable.

Conversation: Darrel Alejandro Holnes & Rickey Laurentiis (February 2013)

After attending a book party for Keith Boykin's anthology For Colored Boys Who Have Considered Suicide When the Rainbow Is Still Not Enough: Coming of Age, Coming Out, and Coming Home *and witnessing various divisions in the LGBT writing community, poets Rickey Laurentiis and Darrel Alejandro Holnes question categorization in today's queer literature and queer literary scene. A casual conversation over Facebook evolved into a longer e-mail correspondence. Here's what these poets had to say:*

Darrel: I was browsing the web searching for new music and stumbled upon this article discussing new, black, gay rap from NYC. This past summer at Cave Canem, a black poetry retreat, other fellows introduced me to the music of Zebra Katz, one of the rappers discussed in this piece. He, along with others, often perform at the Highline Ballroom in the long tradition of ballroom culture, from which vogueing comes. Though it feels as though I'm adjacent to this world, in the city, it's not exactly my own. And this got me thinking, there are so many divisions in Queerdom, categories perhaps to give each sub-group their place on the stage, but do these divisions also block us from seeing outside our own category? What do you think?

Rickey: It's quite interesting and exciting to think about these sort of "queer intrusions," especially those happening in spaces assumed to be exclusively heteronormative or, worse, explicitly violent against queerness. I'm reminded about the queer hip-hop tradition I grew up with back home in New Orleans, about "Sissy Bounce." But there I wonder if the word "intrusion" isn't appropriate, since that music was always already so prevalent. One would literally

hear it thumping on any given corner during a block party
in summer, regardless, it would seem, of the sexuality of
those in attendance. I'm sure there were divisions, but
there was also some greater collectivity happening. Maybe
that just speaks to the possibility of art and entertainment.
So I guess, before I can answer your question, I'd like to
know a bit more about your thoughts about "divisions
in Queerdom," as you put it. Where have you seen them
occur?

Darrel: I see them all around me, whether it be on the club
scene; perhaps more so internationally than in NYC, but
still they're everywhere. When summering in the Canary
Islands with a friend, we were club-hopping and passed by
a leather bar I couldn't enter wearing my cotton striped
tank top—it had to be leather or skin—so I took my shirt
off and walked inside to support my friend's curiosity in
the bar. Though seemingly superficial, the club exercised
a prejudiced commercial practice we would never tolerate
stateside, but it gave the leather daddies a private space in
which they could come together and celebrate their point
of view, celebrate their "beautiful." It was their place in
the spotlight, their place on stage.

I see this in NYC, literary journals, reading series,
performance showcases, and the like only featuring
writers of certain pedigrees; whether it be an unspoken
understanding that to enter you must have an MFA, or
be young, or be black, or have a slam background. These
defined lines help to unite its micro-community members
under one roof. And it's great to be new to the city, as
everyone is at one point, and find your people when they
come together under one roof for different events. There
are so many clubs, crews, and crowds that the categories
help index and make NYC's diversity a manageable delight
instead of a maze of mass confusion.

We see this in literature, too. Right? That division between The Nuyorican Poet's Cafe Poetry Slam and *The Best American Poetry* Reading. Few poets, though more and more do every year, bridge the two worlds. And so on. Wouldn't you say?

Rickey: But I wonder, though, if that kind of behavior isn't tolerated in the States. I'm sure there are more than a few LGBT people here, myself included, who've had some similar experiences at various establishments, whether based on clothing, race, body type, age or what have you. But, you know, your last point about divisions is interesting to me: that while they can risk being problematically exclusionary, segregating one group from another, they can also outline a designated space—a safe space, if you will—where any given community can have its moment to be in the center as opposed to the margins.

And you're absolutely right about these sorts of lines traveling among the writerly community as well. The thing about NYC—and perhaps I have greater clarity because I'm not from there and am not currently living there either—the thing about NYC is that the population itself is already so large, so expansive. If we just think about writers alone, I think it's possible to find one on every block if you just ask! Having lived in the Midwest for about two years now to complete my MFA, I've seen my own writing community—while it has deepened in ways—decrease in literal size. Fewer writers, but (maybe because of that) we all hang out together, are always around each other. So, I guess I'm thinking now that any divisions one sees appearing, any sort of lines, are predicated at some level on a kind of privilege of mass. And that is a kind of privilege, right? To have options, choices, a real visible community around you where you don't feel like you're the only one or one of few? I'm thinking about the leather bar in St.

Louis now, and how—while it's clear I'm not exactly the *imagined* clientele—I did feel as if I was nevertheless welcomed in with some sort of attitude of "the more the merrier." Conversely, it's been in supposedly "progressive" places like NYC, Chicago, and even home in New Orleans where I've had some of my less-than-pleasing experiences, times when I felt like I was being purposefully excluded or impeded. It's a double-edged sword then, right? Categories, divisions, lines. But you say they've made your time in NYC "manageable." What do you mean?

Darrel: For an out-of-towner, let alone a member of the international community, navigating diversity is a (welcome) challenge in NYC. Almost all of my first New York friends and family (mostly white, straight, and privileged) lived in Manhattan. And though I'd see the city's diversity surrounding me when walking to and from work every day, NYC's diversity was mostly off to other boroughs at night, and even those in Harlem or Chinatown were off to locales away from my beaten path. It took developing a more diverse network of friends to be led by others to more homegrown local spots where I could find my Boricua queers (Hombres) and my ballroom black gays (the High Line) or my alternaboys (Westway), etcetera, in nightlife.

I remember one day in NYC it seemed everything was going wrong, and I looked at my community of supporters and realized each one could relate to a different part of my struggle but none could relate to it as a whole. I was sitting in a Burger King in Times Square (the one time in my life) and a troop of fierce, black, queer twenty-somethings entered the restaurant. I couldn't stop staring and even let them in front of me to order so I could watch them walk out. I then asked myself, where is *this* NYC? I love Meatpacking, but there is so much more to me than that crowd. I needed my people; I needed their safety, so I sought them out, gathered in unnamed speakeasies, pop-up parties, karaoke bars, gallery auctions, book clubs, art salons, and the like, on the grind.

Since moving here I've become a member of various niche clubs, organizations, fellowships, boards, and committees that have been starting points for me meeting persons who've become strong and important folks in my inner circle, persons who helped me see that I belonged somewhere in this cutthroat, dog-eat-dog, mess of a place. And some of these groups are unofficial ones, too, a crew of commuters you find when taking the train daily, or a pack of nomad soccer players every Tuesday evening in Central Park.

It's the same in the literary and arts communities, after readings and book parties, you can also find your *you*. But it's easy to see ways in which these niche groups can also be limiting. Take Beauty-Gate (as so dubbed by C. Dale Young), for example. There are a lot of politics involved in making a guest list. So yes, it's definitely a double-edged sword. "Privilege."

Rickey: There are a lot of politics involved in making a guest list, but that practice doesn't seem too different from, say, editing an anthology or even composing a course syllabus. Aren't those all "guest lists" of a kind? For instance, last August, I was at Keith Boykin's book release party in NYC. I was there visiting a good friend of mine, and together we had decided to spend one of our evenings at SPLASH, which was the club hosting the release of *For Colored Boys*. That it was in a club was very interesting. I guess it was an attempt to mesh both public and private, or rather public and "academic." But even as that kind of meshing was going on, I couldn't help but be a little perturbed by, in one sense, the "guest list" being anthologized. Not that I had any special issue with any of those selected (the anthology, I want to stress here, is quite important and gives needed voice to a community), but that I was aware of the divisions: mainly this arbitrary line between "activist" gay writers and their "literary" counterparts or, maybe better said, "performative" and "academic" writers.

Of course, these lines, as we've been saying, were already drawn prior to Boykin's event. But I'm always interested in erasing lines or, at the least, drawing new ones. It may be my own selfish wish, but I wish I had seen a poet like Jericho Brown both on that stage and in Boykin's book, not as a means of trying to push out any other writer who has been selected, but as a means of bridging these large gaps that are so painfully obvious. I think it can be useful, potentially radical, and always interesting to have someone who speaks in (or, maybe better put, to) the "ivory tower" with someone who speaks from (or, again, to) "the street." I've been putting everything in these quotes because none of these terms are exactly stable, none of them quite fit.

When I think of the audience of Boykin's event, that's when I begin to see my desires actualized. For it was in that audience where I saw many I recognized, many who I know either have or are completing graduate degrees, some at Ivy League schools. Some others were men who teach in public high schools. Some, like me, were in the process of getting their MFAs. I'm sure more than a few were only there to hear some good writing and then to dance (and dance they did!). Some further still had 9-to-5s.

It seems as if the audience itself was an anthology: a vast collection of various voices and perspectives, still connected by identity (in that case, their queerness and their black or brownness), but individual as well. Could we say just the meeting of all of us, our literal bodies and our conversations, was a performance of a new knowledge? That's precisely what I think is possible, and the radical potential, of bringing groups together. In the first place, it's a move toward breaking down, at least augmenting, these arbitrary binaries, thereby allowing writers of all kinds to actually see their relationships, to see how we're similar. But what's more interesting, for me, is how bringing various groups together can also reveal our differences, where we diverge individually, within a framework that understands that *that's okay*, that resists assimilation. It's like what's possible of a good classroom debate, insofar as the various opinions, agreements, and disagreements brought together—that kind of easy combination and, yes, hard collision can be a means of discovering, even creating, new ways of understanding, seeing, thinking, and relating. For writers, it could mean new approaches to old themes, for instance, or the adoption of new aesthetics or formal strategies entirely. What's perhaps so often a problem with separate groups as they currently exist is that they can often only recycle, regurgitate, and rehearse the same knowledge, again and again, rarely challenging themselves toward these new kinds of epistemologies. I think if it's possible to wipe the poison off at all, this cross-pollination may be a gesture toward it. It seemed to happen somewhat organically for that audience. Now how do we make our salons, our anthologies, and our course syllabi reflective of that audience?

Darrel: Boykin's book party is a terrific example of niche communities coming together across the same lines that may have boxed other writers out of the anthology itself. I think programming is important. When I was the Programs Director of the Poetry Society of America, I made it my duty to make a case for programming that blurred literary lines and championed diversity; though the efforts were often met with significant resistance, sometimes all you can do is try.

But programming is often so space-oriented that, like theater, it becomes ephemeral, and its value is only relative to those who were able to attend. I'm more interested in considering ways we can create and archive conversations across communities. These days, the largest platform for these conversations is online. And though the jury is out on the success of streaming events, YouTube poetry readings and using more dynamic systems like social networking sites and blogs seem to be the best way to foster intergenerational, cross-disciplinary, and transcultural dialogues. And that's why I've always worked thinking about the importance of "the archive" in various projects throughout my career. One such is Red, White, & Blue: Poets on Politics, an online archive of poets responding to the state of the union and the state of poetry by answering my questionnaire. I learned of the importance of the archive in anthropology courses in graduate school and while developing projects with folklorists across the country. With online archives, anyone across the world can access, and in some cases even contribute, regardless of their location. Having grown up abroad, I always have my eye toward the global community.

The two largest audiences at my public programs this past year were the over 700 in attendance at Cooper Union and the various events I hosted at the Association of Writers and Writing Programs (AWP) annual conference, which played to an audience of around that much as well. Though the programs were well-attended, how many more accessed the recordings online through the *New Yorker* blog and the Poetry Foundation's podcast? How many readers will you and I now have on a site that receives over 100,000 unique clicks a day versus at a literary salon? Add to that readers after the article is shared via Twitter, Facebook, Tumblr, and the like and you'll see that the widest audiences are truly online.

Perhaps what I'm saying is that the best "guest list" in the world of arts and culture is to post an open invitation so all can join the ongoing party. You mentioned how terms like "activist" and "literary" aren't fixed. I'll add to that. Perhaps we shouldn't think of dialogues as fixed within a particular anthology or event. Boykin's book party, for example, might have been an introduction for one or more of its "ivory tower" attendees to the world of queer "street" literature of color, but the exchange continues beyond that introduction. Online, it doesn't matter where you are, or if you arrive late, as long as at some point you get into the party. But then again, you also have to know the party itself is taking place. So it's a bit of a catch-22.

I get around it because I always assume people are talking about interesting things. And that's a consequence of my higher education. As an educator now, teaching creative writing at Rutgers University, I constantly try to show my students that their work, questions, contemplations, and conversations are part of ongoing dialogues, not only in the academy, but also "on the streets." And that there's always a way to include everyone in the conversation; everyone has their place on the stage.

That's how we try to take the "ivory" out of the "tower" in academia. How does the reverse happen in the activist or performance "street" community, and elsewhere? What else can we do to wipe poison from the bad side of the blade?

Rickey: The Internet surely does provide us with a unique database to make these seemingly infinite connections, though it also seems to me that the Internet is only doing what any anthology purports to do but in extreme form: bringing together different, maybe radically different, voices that nonetheless have some connections. Of course, we lose page or other material limitations on the Internet. Doing this kind of work online still requires editorial or curatorial work, right? There still needs to be an administrator. Archiving conversations across communities requires one person (or a team of people) who needs to know of those conversations and communities in the first place. There needs to be one who, for example, knows of Keith Boykin and the work he's doing and of Jericho Brown and his work well enough to know to present them, to link them all, and how best to link them.

That's a little bit about what it comes to for me: who are the editors, how do we make and train more editors, and how do we put these editors in communication with each other so that they may share their lists of writers, thinkers, and artists toward making the kind of audience I described earlier. Every editor inevitably has her or his blind spots, and those blind spots are not always an intention to exclude even if that's the ultimate cost. To spur more conversation I'm sure we need to guard against that kind of blindness toward a more productive re-visioning of community.

But I have questions about your thoughts that the best "guest list" in the world is an open invitation. Is it an open invitation to *participate* or to simply *witness*? There's a difference, no? For the latter, yes, it seems as if any number could do that. Hundreds or more can come to read, agree, comment on this very conversation we're having, but how practical is it that—even on the Internet—the same number could participate? We've created lines right now around ourselves by speaking to ourselves. But this comes back to some of your previous thoughts about the productive purpose of lines. Like in the leather bar, perhaps creating some restrictions enables and produces the kind of safe environment from which true conversation and camaraderie springs. It's for this reason private salons, selective anthologies, parties, events, and what have you don't, in and of themselves, bother me: it's important, I think, to carve out one's individual space for a particular purpose. The issue arises when those individual spaces seem to dominate all conversation, or if not this, the reality of them being the only one or one of few makes it seem like that's the case. So, in my mind, it's not about wiping the poison off—again, I'm not sure how possible that really is—but it's about handling the poison, so to speak. Making it productive.

Darrel: It's an open invitation to participate and witness. Though I see the necessity for curators, editors, and the like, I'm also hesitant to grant sole authority to anyone to solely define a community. Communities are always influx and to define them at any instance is limiting. It's a bit daring, but I instead prefer open forums of evolving conversation, like a Tumblr anthology where anyone can participate or witness; rather than a volume designed with a fixed representation in mind.

I think about Stephen Boyer, who is the manager of the Occupy Wall Street Poetry Anthology. He spearheaded the book project and coordinated the volume's printing and distribution. He also fundraised and promoted the collection. But according to my conversations with him, he never presumed any editorial authority to reject submissions to the anthology and thus "curate" the volume of evolving voices to anything other than a snapshot of responses to the movement in poetry at that time. And now the anthology itself continues to grow beyond its first printed edition.

As we move forward to try to foster more intersectional

dialogue between the "tower" and "the streets," I hope we keep in mind that we can't vest the value of a conversation in the structure of the exchange, but rather in the quality of the content exchanged. I find many anthologies today to be too limiting, too aspiring to be like Norton anthologies which still vibe off the concept of a literary canon. We've been there and done that, time to continue the dialogues on more open platforms like the Internet and social media.

Yes, I did start out talking about the value of drawing lines, but will add that online, this conversation right now can be tagged, shared, and otherwise extended to like conversations in other arts, and outside Literary Queerdom or the overall Queerosphere. When readers follow connecting trends or links, they'll see that anything we say here is meant to *continue* ongoing conversations at the intersections of various disciplines and communities, rather than *be* the sole or most "important" conversation. And I think if we all think of what we write in this way, then we'll be more open to including more voices in the conversation because we'll see it doesn't threaten the place of our own voice on the stage.

You made a point about others needing to know that Boykin and Brown are playing the same game, to even put them in the same league, and that editors ought to lead the way. My point now says the reader has more responsibility to take advantage of the links or avenues, a platform that the Internet provides. We should look at any group and always ask: Who is missing? Why? And what might those missing have to say?

The more curious and demanding the reader, the more boundary-breaking these anthologies, online or in-print, will become. I learned to question during my time in the tower (and at home), but plenty of folks learn to question during their time in the streets, and both are just as valid as long as we continue to challenge the authority's "authority."

I think when you were reading Boykin's book you might have looked and wished Jericho Brown was in there because when reading it you were looking for a voice like your own, and though I'm sure there were plenty in Boykin's book you could relate to, weren't you also scanning the picture for the most recognizable reflection? If we all did that to collections designed to represent "us" there'd be more pressure on editors to meet our thirst for more; as opposed to them just assuming what we want to read, they'd know.

When the National Portrait Gallery recently put together their controversial exhibit of LGBT art, "Hide/Seek," I was shocked at the lack of diversity in the show; so few artists of color, so few female and trans artists. Once more, to be queer meant to be gay, white, and male in America—and the excuse was that the focus was on "canonical artists." You have to raise your voice and say something. If not, so many important voices, whether or not they're your own, won't have a part in the conversation.

Challenge authority, and that also means challenge ourselves. Questioning oneself is often the hardest, though most crucial, part. But by challenging ourselves to practice what we preach to others, we empower ourselves to act and provoke real change. As Junot Díaz pointed out recently when speaking on "decolonizing love," it's a difficult task:

> You grow up and you live a life where you feel like you haven't had shit, the last thing you want to give up is the one thing, the couple of things that you've really held on to. [. . . But] We are never going to get anywhere as long as our economies of attraction continue to resemble, more or less, the economy of attraction of white supremacy.

We have to be critical of others but also of our own selves. Reader, ask yourself how are you diversifying your own personal anthologies? Then seek out poetry and fiction and plays and companionship from communities that are lacking in your life. And then share this work with others online and elsewhere. This, and not just a better-edited Oxford anthology, is the future.

CONVERSATION: DARNELL L. MOORE
& L. LAMAR WILSON (MARCH 2013)

Darnell: Let's begin with your context—that which informs your work, your walk: Who are you?

Lamar: I am an introvert who overanalyzes everything. I am a man of many words, words that are just enough for saying what I must say my way, though they may be excessive to some. Thank God for Gwendolyn Brooks, June Jordan, Brenda Marie Osbey, Thylias Moss, Claudia Rankine, and other masters of the long lyric line and long poem. A good epic is hard to find.

I am prone to tell on myself. The first words in the first poem in *Sacrilegion* say a lot about me: "I talk too much."

Darnell: Where are you from? What life experiences tend to register in your writing?

Lamar: I have three spaces in three cities I must account for each month, but home will always be that modest brick house on that expansive farm in that quiet, North Florida hamlet, Marianna, where acres upon acres of land lie fallow. It's been in my post-Emancipation family for about five generations.

I am one who gets asked "pray for me" a lot, but who is rarely offered prayer, except by elderly women, of whom there aren't enough in my life these days. Those dearly departed raised me well, though, so I oblige the seekers. I was raised to have a healthy Jesus complex; being "like Jesus" (which I deduced as having to be "perfect" at everything I did) was my number one priority for far too long. On the one hand, I got what I prayed for: I've literally been told, "You remind me of black Jesus," for most of my young adult life, especially the last 12 years of growing interlocked hair that now slaps the small of my back as I walk. Men moving in to kiss me and strangers riddled with chemical addictions alike have called me Jesus. Funny, though, not many church folk have noted the resemblance since I told them I kiss men amorously, which didn't start happening until I was of legal drinking age, by the way. (Alas, I'm a recovering prude, or, as is politically correct to say, a very late bloomer.)

The exceptions, of course, are queer men in the black churches in which I've grown up. We are a legion of Jesus freaks. We commit what those who don't understand call sacrilege. We can't help it. Many of my lovers have, in fact, been ministers and have said, "Don't tell nobody." Most have said, "I can't fuck Jesus" only to invert those words and beg for me to be their bodies' lord and savior in a matter of minutes, if only for one night. All have ended up slinking away in shame, hours, days, weeks later. Most have said they weren't married; it took a while for me to discern when one was lying. The bold have brandished their bands, which keeps at least some people from asking questions. Not me. I ask. They usually balk when I tell them I don't get down with mendacity. I *can*, however, be naïve, or at least I know how to pretend to be when the yen for touch calls. You see, that spiritual desire that drives the human mind will lead it to lie to the flesh, tell it what it doesn't deserve, shouldn't taste, shouldn't want, but the flesh is strong and will have its way.

At the center of every poem I wrote in *Sacrilegion*, then, is an intense desire to articulate this yearning to feel both the love of a divine force, which the Greeks call *agape*, and the love of another human's touch, which we know as *eros*. To love, as I was taught, everybody. To want to love on every body you meet, and not all sexually, either. To be, daresay, polyamorous. To embrace the complexity of what that means. To this end, I am a womanist. I prefer this to "black male feminist." I feel no need to affirm my masculinity in owning my love of the Colored, mannish women who reared me, whose spirit I carry with me everywhere I go. I found a deeper love of God and self in embracing Alice Walker's lessons in *In Search of Our Mother's Gardens* and Audre Lorde's "Uses of the Erotic."

But here's where my art-making gets tricky. My flesh—which encodes and signifies the physical elements of my holy, erotic power—is abled differently. Because of a congenital condition, Erb's palsy, I have to do with one hand what others do with two. It took 30 years to own this (dis)ability; I mean, I explained it away at every turn when I was unsuccessful at hiding it. Saying I was "paralyzed" made it true, and my family and I vowed never to own any weakness. Which goes part and parcel, I suspect, with how my ancestors had the unmitigated gall to march into banks and keep buying more of what they knew would give their children's children the ultimate freedom: acres of land, a queer, black space free of the white, patriarchal gaze, with all of its guilt and shame. I call it odd, queer, because in it there was no guilt or shame for my differently-abled flesh. Outside that space, however, I was verbally assailed mercilessly, in large part, ironically, by other brown and black boys and men. But I am prone, like my grandmother and her grandmother, to arrogant behavior, to doing that which others say I can't or shouldn't, based on the limitations they perceive in my way.

Darnell: *Sacrilegion*, then, is a collection of formal and free-verse poetic movements and lyrical ballads organized around notions of embodiment, transcendence, place, race, and sexuality. What was your vision for the book?

Lamar: *Sacrilegion* is an exorcism of the "demons" of perfectionism and respectability, the necessary evils that gave my people a semblance of freedom. And here I mean my nuclear family, who had the audacity to buy the land on which their people had been slaves, and my greater African American families, particularly my Southern black hyper-religious families, who had the audacity to sing into being a belief in Jesus that was co-determinant with a belief in their own liberation, to say, "White America, you've been using God's name in vain; let me show you what my Jesus can do." In this way, these "demons" were once necessary components for our collective sense of spiritual wholeness in a time when we were deemed subhuman, second-class citizens. We decided they were essential for us to plumb the depths of *agape* and *eros* at our disposal so that we might be Jesus' ambassadors in a wicked, oppressive world.

Sacrilegion is obsessed with what was an unspoken, haunting conundrum for so long in my life and in the lives of my people, and it dares my families to go with its speakers into this very queer space in which we find our twenty-first century lives. Far too many of my cosmopolitan, self-aggrandizing loved ones think they must be "post-_____ (black? Southern? religious?)" to keep their faiths and queerness private, in order to actualize an American consciousness unhinged by the specter of chattel slavery and this persistent strain of homophobia that *agape* and *eros* have yet to cure. *Sacrilegion* probes its speakers' journeys—ones very close to mine, others historical, all (re)imagined, some fictively—with hubris and humiliation, those dichotomous realities that manifest in flesh not unlike my own, which is at once revered as holy and reviled as undesirable.

Darnell: What "work" do you expect the book to do in the world?

Lamar: I want it to be widely legible. From its title—which can be pronounced, I pray, at least two ways—to each poem inside its covers, *Sacrilegion* is invested in the tactility and plasticity of America's languages, not only the Southern black Englishes I grew up speaking, but also Spanish, Spanglish, Yoruba, and other African diasporic tongues that have (re)shaped ours. I was recently interviewed by students in Romania, who had discovered my poems through playwright and scholar Rebecca Nesvet, a mutual friend in my Ph.D. program, and I was amazed at the extent to which they got how religious oppression makes one feel, that what I articulated of my rural U.S. southern experience with God resonated with their Eastern European experiences with the divine.

In this way, what I mean, more simply, is that I want to be accessible to the church people I grew up loving, who don't normally engage poetry, to penetrate their mental blocks and social bubbles, and to resonate with scholarly, MFA-friendly readers, who often eschew emotionally transparent, "confessional," religious verse. Hopefully, all will see and feel the implicit complexities in the poems and their speakers' subject positions. I hope I am pushing forward a long-standing tradition of conversations with the idealized/idolized divine, conversations that were once quite common in poetry.

Most of all, I pray that *Sacrilegion* lets my queer, black, (dis) abled, and faith-filled families know someone is out here on the battlefield, telling his truths and hopefully offering a glimpse of theirs, too.

Finally, as I've said in other interviews, the specter of HIV/ AIDS has haunted me most of my life. As a child, I watched it destroy loved ones and watched other's humanity be destroyed by their fear and loathing of what they didn't understand. And in this nation that is insistent upon policing black male flesh—of making black men guilty until proven innocent of a crime—we have legalized ignorance and fear of those men who choose to experience *eros* with other men and keep those choices private. As much as we want to say that this "Know Your Status" campaign is an epistemology of empowerment, it is equally a "Prove Your Innocence" campaign. As current laws in many states stand, those living with this virus and its illnesses are in peril of being found guilty of attempted murder at any moment someone says, "S/he didn't tell me." Emerging in a twenty-first-century moment that is so steeped in the rhetoric of hope around this virus, *Sacrilegion* aims to articulate how it feels to contend with the cruel optimism one deemed a potential criminal knows intimately.

It is my hope that my work forces us to face our fears of HIV/AIDS. Life has brought me intimately close to facing my own, and I hope *Sacrilegion* gives readers their own sublime experience in the mirror.

Darnell: You've noted elsewhere that the writing of poetry is one of your "obsessions." Can you say more about poetry's force in your life and its enchanting power?

Lamar: The economy that writing poetry requires has helped me get out of the way of my words and has transformed what I learned in the church, the missionary impulse, into an act of witness(ing). Everything I feel I need to explain here, in this prose, is palpable in my poems without explanation. That's why I return to poetry, its forms and formal irreverence, early and often. Writing poetry, and *Sacrilegion* in particular, has affirmed this truth I cling to with an exacting certainty: Every body, all flesh, is a mirror, and, as Mama and Daddy taught me, a mirror is a terrible thing to waste.

You see, I have always been a voyeur, and I have almost always loved looking at my naked flesh in mirrors. This important lesson—of knowing one's flesh is a mirror image of the multifaceted divine—is the reason I only embrace my complex ontology as a gift now. For years, I walked through this world feeling cursed by my polyamorous Jesus complex, by my paralysis, by this unwelcome companion; many of my kindred that I encounter still do. Writing *Sacrilegion* helped me excavate the feeling of being blessed with a curse.

Darnell: Which poets inspire you? And, which, if any, helped to shaped *Sacrilegion*?

Lamar: Mrs. Mable Banks, Mrs. Nellie Hubbard, Mrs. Lola M. Cason, and my dearest beloveds, Eldorado Marie "Tudda" Long Grandberry Smith and Mary "MaMary" Elizabeth Long Wilson, laid such a firm foundation and gave me a clear charge to keep. These women, who never spoke of a desire to be known beyond Jackson County, Florida, knew how to tell a story, how to pace their voices and where to put the emphasis, which we call "your weight" back home. They taught me well. As for my formal education, "Resurrection Sunday" and "Substantia Nigra," two of the most important poems in the book for me, would not have been written had I not read Helene Johnson's "A Southern Road." Lucille Clifton's *The Book of Light* and *Mercy* and the personae of our African American master-ventriloquists (Ai, Sterling Brown, Fenton Johnson, and James Weldon Johnson) gave me the courage to commit sacrilege: to re-imagine Lot's daughters as incest victims, not perpetrators, as it is written in our alleged Good Book; to empathize with a sex worker turned sociopathic murderer; to consider HIV a contemporary legion wandering through this wasteland, this graveyard that is post-1980s black America, looking for mirrors, hungry for God's love, too.

Sacrilegion would not exist without the ambivalent horror in Lucy Terry Prince's "Bars Fight," without *Poems on Various Subjects, Religions & Moral* and Phillis Wheatley's exegetical interventions in it, without Frances Ellen Watkins Harper's Aunt Chloe poems. Gary Fisher's posthumous musings (thank you, Eve Sedgwick!), Essex Hemphill's *Ceremonies*, and Melvin Dixon's *Love's Instruments* especially paved the way for this book. As much as I love Elizabeth Alexander's poetry and essays, I love her most for making sure Dixon's voice has a life after his untimely death. Nikki Giovanni's *The Women and the Men*, Marilyn Nelson's *The Homeplace* and *Mama's Promises*, Moss's *Rainbow Remnants in Rock Bottom Ghetto Sky*, Rita Dove's *Mother Love*, Yusef Komunyakaa's *Magic City*, Rankine's *The End of the Alphabet*, and Mary Oliver's *Thirst* are as vital to me as Sharon Olds's *Satan Says*, Marie Howe's *What the Living Do*, D.A. Powell's *Tea*, and Rilke's *Book of Hours*, which gave *Sacrilegion* its epigraph. I love H.D.'s *Hymen*, all things Elizabeth Bishop and Anne Sexton, especially the latter's "The Ballad of the Lonely Masturbator." I love *String Light* by C.D. Wright. I love Fred Moten's *B. Jenkins* and W.S. Merwin's *The Pupil*, all that e.e. cummings, Harryette Mullen, and Ed Roberson have given us. I could go on and on about the books I read in the four years I worked on *Sacrilegion*, all of which I cherish and keep near at all times. I am an insatiable, voracious bibliophile.

Darnell L. Moore is a writer and activist who lives in Bed-Stuy, Brooklyn, USA.

CONVERSATION: SAEED JONES, "OVER COFFEE WITH MELVIN DIXON" (NOV. 2011)

*"If you must leave us, now or later,
the sea will bring you back."*

– Melvin Dixon, "Land's End"

In her introduction to *Love's Instruments*, Melvin Dixon's posthumous poetry collection, Elizabeth Alexander notes:

AIDS has, of course, defined and devastated our times, and the ranks of artists and people of color have been particularly decimated. When literary historians try to write the story of gay black poetry in the late twentieth century, it will be a history swathed with absence.

A peculiar breed of grief sets in when I read and re-read those sentences, and the only way I can describe it is to turn, for a moment, to a parallel universe.

In that universe, we have not lost writers like Melvin Dixon, Essex Hemphill, Joseph Beam, Assotto Saint, Reginald Shepherd, so forth and so on. They are still making art. And, more significantly, they have reached the point in their careers in which they are now able to open doors for emerging queer artists. They are mentors now. Some have created presses and reading series. Others sit on the judging committees of book contests or direct writing programs. Perhaps Melvin Dixon, at this very moment, takes another sip of coffee, arches an eyebrow at the young writer sitting across the table from him, and says, "Baby, what do you mean you haven't heard of Bruce Nugent?" The young writer blushes, then writes down "Smoke, Lilies and Jade" in his notebook, promising to read it as soon as he can get to the library.

Of course, we are not in that parallel universe with them. We are here, doing our best to raise ourselves and each other with the words and art they left behind. In the face of their absence, queer mentorship then takes on a deeper resonance. It is more than a good idea, or the right thing to do; it is a radical act of community building/re-building.

Consider the astounding work Sarah Schulman has done over the course of her career and then remember that Audre Lorde was Schulman's teacher and mentor. How fortunate we all are that Lorde invested her wisdom in Schulman and countless other artists, then left those artists to us.

In graduate school, I was ten minutes into my first poetry workshop with Rigoberto González when it dawned on me that this was the first time in my life I was being taught by a man of color. A queer man of color at that. González's insight in the classroom changed my writing life in ways that I am still processing, but more importantly, he mentored me outside of the classroom as well: inviting me to attend readings with him, urging me to get in touch with other queer poets in New York, and, in fact, I didn't even know Lambda Literary existed until he told me about the foundation. I am deeply grateful for his presence in my writing life, but this would not have happened if I hadn't pursued my MFA. Imagine an arts community in which such mentors were to be found inside as well as outside of MFA programs. In fact, it would be interesting to survey writers to see how many of us have come across lasting mentors entirely outside of academia. The Queer Art Mentorship Fellowship, recently founded by Ira Sachs and Lily Binns, is a pioneering effort to bridge this gap. As a 2011 fellow in the program who has been paired with none other than

Sarah Schulman, I hope to see and join more efforts like this moving forward.

Supporting oneself as an artist is difficult at any stage. And so it is with deep gratitude and more than a bit of awe that I reflect on writers who, in the midst of their day-to-day grind, invest time in speaking to the absence of that lost generation by raising emerging artists. In fact, I would love for you to share your own experiences with queer mentors. Who has helped you write your way into this world?

NOTES

Laurentiis, "Cadaver" was previously published in *Transition*; "Black Iris" in *Vinyl*; "Vanitas with Negro Boy" in *The Paris-American*; and "This Pair This Marriage of Two" in *Callaloo* as "Late Meditation."

Williams, "Sonnet With a Slit Wrist and Flies" was previously published by *The Rumpus*.

Holnes, "Cristo Negro de Portobelo" (The Black Christ of Portobelo) is a celebrated Catholic icon in the town of Portobelo, Panama, that is thought to have existed since 1658. In "The Down Low Messiahs," the line, "In his hands I was a cup overflowing with thirst," is from Eduardo C. Corral's "Our Completion: Oil on Wood: Tino Rodríguez: 1999." This poem was previously published in *Assaracus*. Several lines of "Phenomenon" reference Adrienne Rich's "Diving into the Wreck." This poem was previously published in *Assaracus*. "Stranger Queen" references T.S. Eliot's "The Waste Land," Allen Ginsberg's "Howl," and Donna Summer's "Last Dance."

Wilson, in "Rape," the italicized lines are direct quotations from Chris Brown's interview with Decca Aitkenhead, published October 4, 2013, in *The Guardian*, in which he disclosed that by age 8, he was a porn aficionado and had had sex with someone he described as a girl, age 14 or 15, in his rural Southern hometown of Tappahannock, Virginia. "After the Verdict: Marshall, N.C., July 15, 2013," Ugandan activist David Kato, who successfully sued a national tabloid for calling for him and 99 other gay people to be killed, was beaten to death with a hammer on January 26, 2011. Marco McMillian, 34, an openly-gay politician who was running for mayor of his hometown of Clarksdale, Mississippi, was slain on February 26, 2013, and was found, having been beaten and burned, the following day. Mark Carson, 32, and a friend were trailed and taunted by Elliott Morales on May 17, 2013, in Greenwich Village before Morales fatally shot Carson in the head. After attending a dance party dressed in female clothing, Dwayne "Gully Queen" Jones, 16, of Irwin, Montego Bay, Jamaica, was beaten, stabbed, shot, and run over by a car on July 21, 2013. He died the next day. "On the Occasion of My Fortunate Escape" was published by *Muzzle*.

Conversations, "Holnes and Laurentiis," "Moore on Wilson," and "Jones on Dixon" first appeared at *Lambda Literary*. Gratitude to William Johnson for his constant support.

Conversations, "Holnes and Laurentiis," "Beauty-Gate" refers to a discussion that played out in 2012 on various websites and blogs that centered around beauty, race, class, aesthetics, and privilege. For more information, see the essay, "Anne Sexton, Aesthetics & the Economy of Beauty" by Jameson Fitzpatrick, as well as reader responses to that piece and a follow-up essay by Saeed Jones, "All the Pretty Ones" as posted at *Lambda Literary*.

THE POETS

RICKEY LAURENTIIS has poems appearing or forthcoming in *Boston Review*, *Kenyon Review*, *Fence*, *The New York Times*, and *Poetry*. He is the recipient of a 2012 Ruth Lilly Poetry Fellowship and a 2013 Creative Writing Fellowship from the National Endowment for the Arts and will travel in summer of 2014 with a fellowship from the Civitella Ranieri Foundation to central Italy. Born and raised in New Orleans, Louisiana, he received his MFA from Washington University in St. Louis, where he was a Chancellor's Graduate Fellow. He currently resides in Brooklyn, New York.

PHILLIP B. WILLIAMS is a native of Chicago, Illinois. He is the author of the chapbooks *Bruised Gospels* (Arts in Bloom Inc., 2011) and *Burn* (YesYes Books, 2013). He is a Cave Canem graduate and received scholarships from Bread Loaf Writers Conference and a 2013 Ruth Lilly Fellowship. His work has appeared or is forthcoming in *Anti-*, *Callaloo*, *Kenyon Review Online*, *Poetry*, *The Southern Review*, *West Branch*, and others. Phillip is currently a Chancellor's Graduate Fellow at Washington University in St. Louis and is working on his MFA in Creative Writing. He is the poetry editor of the online journal *Vinyl Poetry*. His full-length debut collection, *Thief in the Interior*, will be published by Alice James Books in 2016.

DARREL ALEJANDRO HOLNES is a writer and producer. He and his work have appeared in *Callaloo*, *The Caribbean Writer*, *Best American Experimental Writing*, *The Best American Poetry* blog, in the Kennedy Center for the Arts College Theater Festival, *TIME Magazine*, *The Feminist Wire*, and elsewhere. He is a Cave Canem Fellow, a Bread Loaf Fellow, and holds degrees in Creative Writing from the University of Michigan and the University of Houston. He currently teaches at Rutgers University, works with the United Nations SRC Society of Writers, and resides in New York.

SAEED JONES received his MFA from Rutgers University–Newark. His work has appeared in publications like *Hayden's Ferry Review*, *StorySouth*, *Jubilat*, and *The Collagist*. He is the LGBT content editor for *Buzzfeed* and is a regular contributor to *Ebony.com* and *Lambda Literary*. His chapbook, *When the Only Light Is Fire*, was published in 2011 by Sibling Rivalry Press and was recognized by the American Library Association as a top-ten favorite through its "Over the Rainbow" list of recommended LGBT reading. In the fall of 2014, Coffee House Press will release his first full-length collection of poems, *Prelude to Bruise*. He's received fellowships from Queer / Arts / Mentorship as well as Cave Canem.

L. LAMAR WILSON is the author of *Sacrilegion* (2013), the 2012 selection for the Carolina Wren Press Poetry Series, an Independent Publishers Group bronze medalist, and a Thom Gunn Award for Gay Poetry finalist. Wilson, a Cave Canem and Callaloo Fellow, holds an MFA from Virginia Polytechnic Institute and State University and is completing a doctorate in African American and multiethnic American poetics at the University of North Carolina at Chapel Hill. Visit him at llamarwilson.com.

JOE MALFETTONE, born in Fairfield County, Connecticut, is a multi-disciplinary conceptual artist. You may learn more at www.joemalf.com. He has designed this piece, titled *Prime*, specifically for this publication.

SIBLING RIVALRY PRESS is an independent publishing house based in Alexander, Arkansas. Our mission is to publish work that, in the words of Adrienne Rich, disturbs and enraptures. [www.siblingrivalrypress.com]

Lightning Source UK Ltd.
Milton Keynes UK
UKOW01f0321240817
307871UK00001B/45/P